Peter and the Wolf

Level 3

Retold by Lynne Doherty Herndon
Series Editor: Melanie Williams

Pearson Education Limited
Pearson
KAO Two
KAO Park
Harlow
Essex
CM17 9NA

and Associated Companies throughout the world.

ISBN 9781292240091

This adaptation first published by
Penguin Books 2003
7 9 10 8
Text copyright © Pearson Education Limited 2003
Illustrations copyright © Rhian Nest James / Kathy Jakeman
page 31, Bridget Dowty / GCI

Retold by Lynne Doherty Herndon
Series Editor: Melanie Williams
Illustration by Rhian Nest James & Bridget Dowty
Design by Wendi Watson

Printed in Great Britain by Ashford Colour Press Ltd.
SWTC/01

The moral right of the author and illustrator have been asserted

Published by Pearson Education Limited

For a complete list of titles available in the Pearson Story Readers series please write
to your local Pearson Education office or contact:
Pearson, KAO Two, KAO Park, Harlow, Essex, CM17 9NA

Answers for the Activities in this book are published in the free Pearson English Story
Readers Factsheet on the website, www.pearsonenglishreaders.com

Once there was a boy named Peter, who lived with his grandfather in a little house behind a red gate. Outside the gate there was a beautiful, green meadow full of tall grass, lovely flowers and friendly animals. Next to the meadow there was a dark, dangerous forest.

Peter's grandfather was an old man, who loved Peter very much. But Peter did not always do what his grandfather told him to do – and that made his grandfather angry!

One morning at breakfast, Peter's grandfather told him, "Remember, Grandson. You must never play in the meadow by yourself."

"Why not, Grandfather?" asked Peter.

"A hungry wolf lives in the forest," his grandfather answered. "He could come out into the meadow and eat you up!"

"Oh, Grandfather!" said Peter. "I'm not afraid of a wolf."

Peter's grandfather shook his head. "You must never play in the meadow by yourself."

The next morning, while his grandfather
was still asleep, Peter opened the gate and
went out into the beautiful, green meadow.
A little, yellow bird sat on a tall tree outside
the gate. The little bird sang happily when
she saw Peter coming through the gate.

"Shh!" whispered Peter. "Grandfather must not know that I am here!"

Just then a fat, white duck came through the gate after Peter. She was happy that the gate was still open, because she wanted to take a nice swim in the meadow's cool pond.

The bird flew down from the tree and started to fly in circles around the duck's head.

"Why must you walk to the pond?" asked the bird. "Why don't you fly like me?"

The duck did not say anything to the bird until she was right next to the pond.

"Why must you fly around the pond?" asked the duck. "Why don't you swim in it like me?" Then she swam happily to the middle of the pond.

"Ha! You don't know how to fly!" cried the bird.

"Ha! You don't know how to swim!" answered the duck.

Peter lay in the warm sun laughing at the bird and the duck. Suddenly he heard a noise. A striped, orange cat was coming through the meadow's tall grass.

"Aha!" thought the cat. "The bird doesn't see me. I'll get her!" Quietly he moved through the grass.

The bird saw the striped, orange cat and flew to the top of the tree.

The cat walked below the tree, looking fiercely at the bird.

"Don't be scared," Peter called to the bird. "The cat cannot get you up there!"

"I'm not afraid of the cat," said the bird.

Grandfather came out of the house. He saw that the gate was open. He saw that Peter was in the meadow.

"Peter!" he said angrily. "I told you that you must never play in the meadow by yourself. If a wolf came out of the forest, what would you do?"

"Oh, Grandfather!" said Peter. "I'm not afraid of a wolf!"

Peter's grandfather shook his head.

"You must never play in the meadow by yourself," he repeated.

He took Peter's hand and walked with him across the green meadow. Then he took Peter into the yard and closed the red gate.

As soon as Peter and his grandfather left
the meadow, a big, gray wolf came out
of the forest. He looked at the bird and
the cat with hungry eyes. The cat was
so afraid that his whiskers shook. He
quickly climbed up the tree, not thinking
about the bird.

The duck was still swimming happily around the pond. She did not see the wolf come out of the forest. The wolf moved quickly and quietly through the tall grass next to the pond. When the duck saw him, she was so afraid that she jumped out of the water!

The duck ran slowly on her flat duck's feet, while the wolf followed quickly on his long, strong legs. Now she was more afraid! The duck tried to run faster, but the wolf was much faster than she was. He was getting nearer and nearer to the poor, fat duck.

Then the wolf caught the duck and ate her.

The wolf saw the bird and the cat in the tree. He walked nearer and looked at them with his hungry eyes. He wanted to eat them, too!

Peter stood in the yard behind the gate, watching everything.

"I'm not afraid of a wolf!" Peter thought. He ran into the house but did not let Grandfather see him. He found a strong piece of rope. He came out to the yard and climbed up the high, stone wall next to the gate. Then he climbed onto the tree.

"Listen, Birdie," Peter whispered. "If you fly in circles around the wolf's head, I can catch him. You can help me but you must be careful – be careful that he doesn't catch you, too!"

"The wolf cannot catch me," whispered the little bird. "I'm not afraid of the wolf!"

The bird flew in quick circles around the
wolf's head. How the wolf wanted to catch
her and eat her up! But the bird was quicker
than he was, and the wolf could not catch
her. Soon, he was so tired that all he wanted
to do was lie down.

Peter knew he had to work fast. He tied one
end of the rope to the tree. Then he tied the
other end of the rope in a circle and threw
it down from the tree. He carefully put the
circle of rope around the wolf's tail.

Then Peter pulled as hard as he could. The wolf jumped angrily, trying to shake the rope off of his tail. But he could not.

"Meow!" said the cat loudly, starting to climb down the tree. The little bird sat happily on Peter's shoulder and looked down at the wolf.

Suddenly, some hunters came out of the forest. They were riding horses through the forest and hunting for the wolf. The hunters saw the wolf in the meadow, but they did not see Peter in the tree. They pulled out their guns and got ready to shoot the wolf.

Peter saw the hunters. He did not want the wolf to hurt them, but he also did not want the hunters to hurt the wolf.

"Don't be afraid!" he told the wolf. "I won't let the hunters shoot you!"

"I'm not afraid of the hunters," said the wolf.

The hunters climbed down from their horses and looked at Peter. Peter was sitting in the tree with the bird and the cat. He still had one end of the piece of rope in his hand. The wolf sat quietly under the tree with the other end around his tail.

"Look!" Peter said. "We have caught the wolf! If you find a cage, we can put him in it and take him to the zoo."

The hunters were surprised to see so clever and brave a boy. They went into the forest and brought back a very big cage.

When the wolf was in the cage, Peter climbed down from the tree with the bird on his shoulder. The cat, still a little afraid of the wolf, quietly followed them.

"Thank you for helping us," Peter said to the hunters. "Now, let's take the wolf to the zoo."

Then Peter's grandfather came out of the house. "I told you that you must never play in the meadow by yourself!" he said angrily. "If a wolf came out of the forest, what would you do?"

"I would catch him," Peter answered. "I'm not afraid of a wolf. Look Grandfather!"

Peter's grandfather could not believe his eyes. Peter was standing in front of a cage with a big, gray wolf inside.

"Don't be afraid," the hunters said. "Your grandson is very clever and brave. He and his friends caught the wolf. Now we're going to take him to the zoo."

Peter walked in front with the little, yellow bird on his shoulder. The hunters followed, carrying the cage with the wolf inside. Then came Grandfather and the striped, orange cat.

"Don't be afraid, Wolf," Peter said. "There's good food to eat in the zoo."

"I'm not afraid," said the wolf.

Activities

Before you read

1. Think about these questions. Write a short answer for each one.

a. The name of this story is "Peter and the Wolf." What is a wolf? Have you ever seen a wolf? Can you think of a story about a wolf? Is the wolf in the story good or bad?

b. Look at the picture on page three of the story. What do you see?

c. Look at the pictures below. Where do you find each animal: in (a) a meadow, (b) a pond or (c) a forest?

After you read

2. Put the sentences from the story in the right order.

a. A striped, orange cat came through the meadow.

b. "Don't be afraid, Wolf," Peter said. "There's good food to eat in the zoo."

c. Peter caught the wolf with a rope.

d. A fat, white duck came through the gate after Peter.

e. Suddenly some hunters came out of the forest.

f. The wolf caught the duck and ate her!

g. The little bird sang happily when she saw Peter coming through the gate.

h. A big, gray wolf came out of the forest.

3. Word search

Here are some words from the story.
Find the words in the word square.

bird   cage

cat   duck

forest   gate

hunter   meadow

pond   wolf

g	l	d	u	c	k	o	p	m
a	a	s	d	f	g	h	j	e
t	k	l	z	x	v	b	n	a
e	w	o	l	f	p	o	n	d
b	i	r	d	o	f	g	h	o
d	s	a	q	r	w	e	c	w
h	u	n	t	e	r	a	a	s
t	y	u	i	s	e	p	g	e
c	a	t	u	t	s	t	e	r